KT-513-483

TIME OUT
IN NewZealand

TIME OUT IN New Zealand

Photographs/Walter Imber
Text/Mervyn Dykes

A.H. & A.W. REED
WELLINGTON SYDNEY LONDON

First published 1979

A.H. & A.W. REED LTD

65-67 Taranaki Street, Wellington
53 Myoora Road, Terrey Hills, Sydney 2084
11 Southampton Row, London WC1B 5HA

16-18 Beresford Street, Auckland
Cnr Mowbray and Thackeray Streets, Waltham, Christchurch

© 1979 A.H. & A.W. Reed Ltd.

All rights reserved. No part of this publication
may be reproduced, stored in a retrieval system or
transmitted in any form or by any means, electronic,
mechanical, photocopying, recording or otherwise,
without the prior written permission of the publishers.

ISBN: 0 589 01135 9

Jacket design and layout by David J. Kingston.
Typesetting by A.H. & A.W. Reed Ltd.
Printed by Dai Nippon Printing Co. (Hong Kong) Ltd.

Contents

Walter Imber, the photographer of *Time Out in New Zealand*, is an internationally-known photographer who works from Berne, Switzerland.

His work has appeared in many European publications and in K.B. Cumberland's book *New Zealand*, also published by A.H. & A.W Reed.

Walter Imber combines the qualities of artist and athlete to achieve his world-class photographs. For this book, he went out on the Bluff oyster boats, flew high over the Marlborough Sounds and Christchurch, donned tramping boots in Fiordland and Northland, ventured into shearing sheds and geyser country, slogged up mountains and down caves. The results are some of the most eye-catching photos ever to be published about this country.

Mervyn Dykes is one of New Zealand's best known journalists, whose knowledge of his native country has few equals. He answers the traveller's questions with hard facts and practical information.

His books include the recently-published *Hauraki Gulf*, for which he wrote the text to John Castle's evocative paintings. He lives in Auckland.

Introduction

NEW ZEALAND is the kind of country that actually fits the cliches coined by travel agencies to bring flocks of tourists migrating to its shores.

The three major islands sprawl for 1500km in the temperate zone of the Southern Hemisphere, but nowhere can you travel more than 110km from a coastline and the pounding of the surf.

It is home to three million humans and more than 56 million sheep. The pioneers called it "God's Own Country". In the travel brochures New Zealand has been billed as a "Pocket Paradise" and a "Scenic Wonderland".

What this means is that in only 26,870.4 hectares (269,360 sq. kilometres), travellers can find glaciers and hot pools, waterfalls and geysers, ice and boiling mud. They can see sky-scraping mountains, deep mysterious fjords and fertile coastal plains.

The more adventurous can stalk chamois, tahr, wild pigs, or several varieties of deer. There are rivers and lakes that yield vigorous rainbow and brown trout. Those called by the sea can seek possible world-record game fish in waters that American writer, Zane Grey, once dubbed "the angler's Eldorado".

Add to this glow-worm caves, first-class ski fields, canyons, and lakes of cathedral stillness. The list is almost endless and the contrasts are many.

In the North Island, travellers can spend a morning soaking up the peace of hill after lush green hill and marvelling at the numbers of sheep or cattle scattered like droplets on the emerald green.

The same day, an easy drive away, they can thrill to the brimstone and barely suppressed fury of thermal areas with names like Hell's Gate and Earthquake Valley.

Down South there is wild high country, scraped bare to reveal nature's strength. Vivid yellows and oranges illuminate the trees on the plains. Rivers at first tumble and scour their paths from the mountains and spread happily into middle-age before they pass over the last sand bar and into the sea.

The Southern Alps rise from the shoulders of the hills like the spines on a dragon's back — more than 20 peaks exceed 3000m in height and several huge glaciers are many kilometres in length.

Across the alps lie almost impenetrable explosions of rain forest and the wild and lonely stretch of the West Coast which still has echoes of pioneer times.

The people of New Zealand show as many contrasts as the land.

Auckland, New Zealand's major city, also boasts the world's largest Polynesian population. Wellington is the nation's capital and diplomatic centre. Christchurch, the largest city in the South Island, has an unmistakable English heritage, and Dunedin in the far south is proud to be Scottish.

As well, there are many smaller pockets where French, Scandinavian, Dalmatian and other European pioneers made their first homes.

Today, 92 per cent of New Zealand's population is of European origin and 7 per cent to 8 per cent are Maoris, a Polynesian people who preceded the pakeha, or white man, by several hundred years.

According to tradition and legend, a great Maori explorer named Kupe was said to have discovered New Zealand about AD 950. In 1350, the Great Fleet of open canoes brought Maori settlers from Hawaiiki, their fabled homeland.

Modern scholars question the arrival of a single fleet, but whatever happened the Maoris came by canoe, steering by the stars through waters that have claimed many ships. They must have covered thousands of miles in one of the world's greatest feats of navigation.

The first European contact with New Zealand was provided by a Dutchman, Abel Tasman, who sailed past the southern tip of Australia and sighted the west coast of the South Island in 1642.

He sailed northward up the coast and returned to Europe not knowing whether he had discovered an island group or part of a great southern continent that scholars suspected must exist.

In 1769, he was followed by an Englishman, Captain James

Cook, who was the first to circumnavigate the North and South Islands. Cook prepared amazingly accurate maps of the new land and his name has been given to the strait which separates the two main islands.

The first explorers found the Maori people living in tribal groupings that had many similarities to the Scottish clans and, to a certain extent, the American Indians.

While the Maoris still used stone tools for carving, construction, agriculture and as weapons in battle, they had a highly-developed society which placed great importance on family groupings.

There was then no written language — genealogies, sagas, and important information were incorporated in chants and painstakingly passed from generation to generation.

A visit to the Maori Court at any of the museums in the main centres will show how traditions and stories were captured in carvings as well.

You will also see models of the pas or fortified villages with their elaborate systems of trenches and stockades.

While New Zealand is well and truly in the 20th century, a flight over Auckland quickly reveals traces of old fortifications on many of the volcanic cones and more prominent hills.

The Maoris may not have had metal tools, but they had the next best thing in greenstone, a hard jade-like rock which, with perseverance and skill, could be shaped and made to take an edge.

Greenstone was also used extensively for ornaments and modern tourists can buy greenstone tikis and other replicas of ancient crafts from souvenir shops. However, there would be considerable opposition to the sale of a genuine, ancient artefact if it was to be taken from the country.

Food was generally prepared in a hangi, or earth oven. Heated river stones were placed at the bottom of a pit and the food, wrapped in damp leaves or matting placed on top. The pit was then filled in and the food left to cook.

The hangi has survived to this day and it is not uncommon for Maoris and pakehas to hold hangis on special occasions — much as people in other countries might hold a barbecue.

Yes (while we are on the subject of ovens), some Maori groups were cannibalistic, devouring members of other tribes captured in battle, or perhaps a wayward European.

A Maori health officer once told a university seminar that he was part Scottish — by absorption.

"My great grandfather ate a missionary," he said. His predominantly pakeha audience laughed.

If the explorers were the first white men to be seen by the Maoris, the exploiters came soon after.

There were sealers and whalers who plied far south for their animal harvests. They have their modern counterparts today in the hundreds of foreign fishing boats — mostly Russian, Japanese, Korean and American — which ring New Zealand's coasts.

Next to interest the Europeans was the land and this was to cause many Maori-Pakeha confrontations. A Maori's land was his life, his heritage, but the settlers also needed land to live.

Finally, the Treaty of Waitangi was signed on February 6, 1840, at the Bay of Islands and the cornerstone of a nation was laid. Today, February 6 is observed as Waitangi Day.

New Zealand is a monarchical state and a member of the British Commonwealth. The Queen of England is the Queen of New Zealand. She is represented in this country by a Governor General, who serves a five-year term.

In 1967 there was a change in the nature of the appointment of governors general. In that year, Sir Arthur Porritt became the first New Zealand-born person to rise to that high office. It has now become accepted that the honour will go to a "true" New Zealander rather than a distinguished Englishman.

The political system is democratic, with a 92-member House of Representatives being elected each three years. While Maoris can stand for election to any of the seats, there can never be a parliament without Maori members because four of the seats are exclusively Maori.

For many years there have been two main political parties — National (Conservative) and Labour. The leader of the majority party in parliament is known as the Prime Minister. He, the ministers in his cabinet and the Governor General form the Executive Council.

In 1893, New Zealand gave women the vote, being beaten in its recognition of women by only Pitcairn Island and the U.S. State of Wyoming. Today, every New Zealander over the age of eighteen has the right to vote.

For most of its history, New Zealand has been dependant on overseas trade, particularly in meat, wool, and dairy products. However, in recent years manufacturing industries have assumed a growing importance.

Even though New Zealand was the last significant habitable land mass to be discovered, it is largely an unknown quantity to many people in the Northern Hemisphere. Americans often confess sheepishly that because of its name they first thought New Zealand was "somewhere in Scandinavia". Others confuse it with Australia — a great insult to a small, but fiercely independent, Pacific nation!

A study of its achievements in the social and physical sciences, sport, and the arts though, makes it clear that New Zealand has made contributions out of all proportion for a country with a total population smaller than that of many overseas cities.

It is often hard to realise that Ernest, later Lord Rutherford, the first person to split the atom, received his early education in the small South Island town of Nelson. There are many modern examples too from Sir William Pickering who reached into space as the head of NASA's Jet Propulsion Laboratory to heart surgeons such as Sir Brian Barratt-Boyes, experts on the unborn child such as Professor Sir William Liley, and a great many agricultural and marine scientists.

New Zealand is particularly well known to sportsmen and women the world over. Its athletes and sports teams are in great demand in the United States of America and Europe.

Mountaineer Sir Edmund Hillary was, along with Tensing Norkay, the first climber to conquer Mt Everest.

Its hockey players captured a gold at the Montreal Olympics. Runner John Walker led the 1500 metres field home there too. The rowing eight beat the world's best "semi-professionals" at Munich and the All Blacks, the national Rugby Union football side, has been a great power on the world scene for most of this century.

However, it is this love of sport — amounting almost to fanaticism in some areas — which prompted the walkout of African nations at the Montreal Olympics. New Zealand's Government had opted not to interfere with the right of sports bodies to play whichever country they pleased. The decision to send the All Blacks to renew the long-standing rivalry with the South African Springbok side was greeted with distaste by Black African nations — a distaste that was shared by sizeable groups within New Zealand.

Along with horse racing and beer drinking, rugby is often jokingly referred to as a major New Zealand religion — it certainly gets a better turnout than most of the churches!

Census statistics show that of those New Zealanders who have no objection to declaring their religious profession 895,839 are Anglicans (Episcopalean), 583,701 are Presbyterian, and 449,974 are Catholic.

Methodists number 182,727, and then there is a drop of more than 140,000 to Baptists, the Church of Jesus Christ of Latter Day Saints (Mormons), and the Ratana Church, which is based on the teachings of a Maori prophet.

About 70 per cent of New Zealand's population lives in the North Island. More than 700,000, or nearly a quarter of the total population, lives in the greater Auckland area.

Auckland is a city with not one but two major natural harbours — the Waitemata and the Manukau. While most major cities in the world climb upward, Auckland in the New Zealand style, sprawls out, taking full advantages of beaches, hillsides, valleys, and even its extinct volcanic cones.

Auckland has a particularly fine museum, one of the two leading art galleries in the Southern Hemisphere, and also a Museum of Transport and Technology which exists as a tribute to the marvellous foresight of citizens who acted to preserve part of their heritage before it was lost forever.

There are fine hotels, motels, restaurants and all the trappings of big cities everywhere. Street wear is casual as befits a semi-subtropical climate where summer falls between November and February. Winter is still relatively warm, but usually a great deal wetter.

Wellington, at the foot of the North Island, has in its area of influence a population of 590,000. The urban area is based on a particularly beautiful natural harbour enclosed by high hills.

It is a fitting site for the nation's capital, the home of the House of Parliament. In the one compact area visitors can see one of the world's largest wooden buildings (the old government building), the massive stone Parliament Building, and the modern beehive-shaped additions supposed by optimists to signify the industry with which the parliamentarians go about their affairs.

Wellington too has a fine museum, the National Art Gallery, and a thriving waterfront which is at once home to large ships and the inevitable small boys who dangle sprat lines from the wharves. A maritime museum can be found there.

Just as Auckland has Takapuna City and the North Shore across the Waitemata, so does Wellington have the Hutt Valley and the twin cities of Upper and Lower Hutt. In Wellington's case, the connection is not by harbour bridge, but by motorway along the fringe of the waterfront. The Hutt Valley houses most of the Capital's industry, as well as studios for the nation's two television channels.

Christchurch, the principal city of the South Island, is a city of parks, gardens, fine stone buildings and the beautiful poplar-lined River Avon which was transformed from a rather scruffy stream by the pioneers.

Much of the flavour of this pioneer life is preserved in a wing of the city's museum — well worth a visit.

Dunedin, the most southern of the main centres, is also a garden city and also based on a port. The first university in New Zealand was founded there in 1869 and it developed special schools in medicine, dentistry, home science, and physical education.

The city is also well known for its architecture, particularly the older buildings which make use of South Island stone. A fine way to take in as many of the city's sights as possible is to follow the "Golden Arrow" scenic drive.

The Alexander Turnbull Library and the National Library

together house a superb collection of rare literary and Pacific manuscripts and books.

With so many natural advantages, it is to be expected that tourism is big business in New Zealand. What is surprising though is that in spite of its relative isolation from the rest of the world New Zealand features regularly in the three or four destinations most popular with travellers.

More than 60 per cent of the visitors to New Zealand come from Australia, with Japan, North America, South-East Asia, and the Pacific Islands accounting for lesser numbers.

There has been a determined attempt to "sell" the special features of the country too. Tours are being "tailor-made" for parties of hunters and fishermen and many New Zealanders have been startled to find out how well-known some of their favourite fishing spots have become overseas.

It seems that the brotherhood of the huntin' — shootin' — fishin' types knows no national boundaries.

As Australia is New Zealand's closest neighbour of any real affluence, it is predictable that Australians should dominate the flow of incoming tourists. However, they enjoy considerable advantages over travellers from other countries. For example, New Zealanders and Australians visiting each others' countries do not require passports or visas.

Anyone wishing to obtain permission to settle in New Zealand, except for Australians, should first write to the nearest representative of the New Zealand Government in their country of origin, or else write direct to the Secretary of Labour, Private Bag, Te Aro, Wellington.

The travel surge to New Zealand has become such that the number of visitors doubles every four or five years. There is a busy stream in the opposite direction as well, for New Zealanders are among the world's most travel-conscious people.

Perhaps it's a result of the relative isolation from the main population centres. Perhaps it's just a national itch. Whatever the reason, young New Zealanders seem to find the challenge of getting to another country irresistible.

Working holidays in Australia and Europe have always been popular and now the more adventurous are turning to overland treks through eastern countries.

Tourists coming to New Zealand are likely to spend more than half of their total outlay on travel to and from their home country.

Once in New Zealand, they will find that transport and accommodation will be their biggest expenses — transport alone will account for some 30 per cent of their spending.

Generally, the standard of transport and accommodation lose nothing in comparison with those in the tourists' home countries.

However, there is still a certain lack of sophistication which many visitors find endearing. The custom of tipping, for example, is still the exception rather than the rule.

Besides the air services, all major centres in New Zealand are connected by sealed roads. Rail traffic, too, is heavy in both the North and the South Island.

Today, the tracks of the national network snake for nearly 5000km through both major islands, with the more populated North Island having slightly more than half of the total.

There are 182 railway tunnels, with an aggregate length of 84.5 kilometres in use — 107 in the North Island and 75 in the South Island. About 2,600 bridges and viaducts have been built, totalling 90 kilometres in length.

The standard gauge is 1067mm and the island systems are connected by a rail and vehicular ferry services across Cook Strait between Wellington in the north and Picton in the south.

One feature of special interest to travellers is the diesel-powered express service operated in the South Island by the Southerner and in the North Island by the Silver Star and the Northerner. With buffet or dining cars, they can be among the most attractive and inexpensive ways of enjoying the magnificent scenery. The Northerner also has sleeping compartments.

Once the main travel lanes are left, there is a well-organised system of light aircraft services by small airlines and aero-clubs — the latter being willing to run charter flights to the more remote or specialised destinations. Often travellers land on alpine glaciers or mountain lakes in their search for the unusual.

There are even many organised tramping trips which pass through remote country, yet are well within the scope of grandparents or as has often been the case, parties of exercise-seeking coronary patients on the mend.

Besides the scenery, the sporting attractions are great.

Big game fishing in the warm waters of the east coast of the North Island provide some of the best surf, line and scuba fishing in the world.

The main bases for line fishing from charter boats are at Whangaroa, Bay of Islands (Russell, Otehei Bay and Waitangi — made famous by Zane Grey), Tutukaka, Mercury Bay (Whitianga), and Mayor Island (Tauranga).

Among the most prized catches are broadbill, black marlin, striped marlin and blue marlin. Other types of big game fish common to New Zealand waters are tiger shark, hammerhead shark, mako shark, thresher shark, kingfish (yellow tail) and tuna. While the best catches are usually made in February, fishing is good from December to April.

In addition there is a wide variety of smaller fish which provide excellent sport.

Fresh water fishing in the lakes, rivers and mountain streams can be just as spectacular. Rainbow and brown trout are the most common species with size varying according to climate, food available and angling pressure.

In the North Island the most popular trout fishing areas are the Rotorua Lakes and the massive Lake Taupo in the centre of the island.

The average trout weights in the North Island are. Rotorua, rainbow 1-1.2kg (2-2½lb), brown, 2.3kg (5lb); Taupo, rainbow 2kg (4½lb) and brown 2.3kg (5lb); river systems, both species about 1kg (2lb).

In the South Island, the average weights are: lake systems, 1-1.4kg (2lb-3lb), both species; sea-run brown trout, 2.3kg (5lb) in west coast rivers; sea-run "Quinnat" salmon, 5.5kg (12lb) in the east coast rivers; land-locked salmon, 1-1.2kg (2lb-2½lb).

As mentioned earlier, much depends on the angling pressure of the region. The more remote areas of the South Island can return some spectacular catches of brown trout well into the double figures.

The author once flew into the Lake McKerrow-Martins Bay area of Fiordland and watched a member of the party catch six brown trout each weighing more than 2.7kg (6lb) in the space of half an hour.

Recent visitors to the area had landed fish which had tipped the scales at 6kg (13½lb) and 8.2kg (18lb). The angler who bagged the 6kg (13½-pounder) had travelled all the way from the United States for his catch and an element of his excitement was recorded in the diary of the tramping hut where he had stayed.

He had scrawled the details of his catch in a shaky hand and rounded up no fewer than six eye-witnesses to give his fishy story substance.

Shooting and bow hunting are both practised in New Zealand with rabbits and deer assuming pest proportions and requiring firm methods of control.

The principal game birds are duck, swan, pheasant, geese, quail, and chukor, but the sport is limited, the season usually extending for about six weeks from early May.

However, there is still no limit on the number of game animals that may be taken. No game licences are required and the season is open all year round.

The top trophies include chamois and tahr, but good hunting is provided by red deer, fallow deer, wild pigs, goats, and wallaby.

Other species present in lesser numbers are wapiti (elk), sambur deer, rusa deer, sika deer, and whitetail deer. A guide is essential for results.

There are even rumours of moose in the remoter reaches of the South Island. Attempts were made to liberate the shy giants there, but the various species of deer were believed to be too competitive.

The search for moose has acquired some of the elements of the hunt for the abominable snowman or yeti in the Himalayas. Some hunters say New Zealand moose don't exist, while others claim to have seen tracks or recent droppings.

Skiing is another popular pastime in New Zealand and is usually enjoyed from mid-July to late October in the North Island and from early July to late September in the South Island.

Determined skiers can enjoy good spring skiing in the South Island by taking ski-planes from the Mt Cook airstrip to the southern glaciers.

In the North Island, the main skiing area is at Mt Ruapehu in the Tongariro National Park. Equipment and instruction is available for skiers and there are four chair-lifts, a T-bar, three Poma lifts, and numerous tow ropes. A new ski field has opened at Turoa, above the township of Ohakune.

Mt Ruapehu is situated in the heart of the volcanic plateau and has distinctive twin peaks, cupping a hot crater lake. Close by are Mt Tongariro and Mt Ngauruhoe — an active volcano. Climbers or photographers with a yen for volcanic scenery should not fail to visit them.

Away to the west in Taranaki province is Mt Egmont, a cone so symmetrical it has been compared to Fujiyama in Japan. There is one main serviced ski area, above Stratford.

In the South Island, the main ski areas are at Mt Cook (a major tourist centre), Coronet Peak near Queenstown (another important tourist spot), Mt Hutt, Lake Ohau, Porters Pass, and Arthur's Pass.

Coronet Peak is 11km (seven miles) from Queenstown and has the best powder snow conditions in New Zealand. It lies on extensive, undulating slopes and boasts a full range of equipment and services.

The volcanic plateau in the central North Island has a startling variety of attractions running the full extent from snowfields to hot mineral springs and boiling mud pools.

Among the popular fishermen's tales is one which at first sounds impossible — catching a trout in one fork of a stream and towing it up another fork to a natural hot spring where it can be cooked on the hook.

Most aspects of the New Zealand way of life have been recorded by writers, photographers, artists and painters in a wide range of first class books — some of which are listed elsewhere in this publication.

In the meantime, let's take a closer look at some of the attractions New Zealand has to offer.

South Island

TE WAKA A MAUI was what the ancient Maoris called the South Island — the canoe of Maui — and Stewart Island at its foot was the anchor stone. The Maori name harkens back to the legend of how Maui fished the North Island out of the sea in the misty, magical past.

For such an undertaking he needed an extraordinary canoe and the one he used is about 800km (500 miles) long and 280km (175 miles) across at its widest point.

The South Island is larger and geographically older than the North Island. The rugged, alpine grandeur of its scenery, the crystal lakes and swift rivers were buried under thousands of feet of ice some 15,000 years ago. Today, even an unskilled eye can read the signs of glacial passage.

Like a dragon's spine, the awesome Southern Alps stretch the length of the island and include the triple-peaked Mt Cook which at 3,764m (12,349ft) is the highest point in New Zealand.

The savage, almost unimaginable beauty of the remoter reaches of the South Island still retain a wierd capacity to suddenly present a scene which startles even the most experienced traveller into thinking of other times, other places, of home — or maybe even of heaven.

Unearthly, primitive, a part of the world that time forgot . . .

12

Tucked away in the south-western corner of the South Island is Fiordland National Park, the fifth largest national park in the world.

In spite of its relative isolation, thousands of visitors stream through Fiordland each year to experience the almost mystical atmosphere of settings that have amazingly remained virginal and unspoiled.

There are many places where visitors can turn their backs on companions and savour the feeling of being alone yet surrounded by a vibrant, natural force.

Milford Sound is a true fjord — the glacier which scooped it out in prehistoric times left a moraine deposit where it meets the sea, so that the seaward entrance is shallower than the head of the fjord. A modern tourist hotel enjoys breathtaking views of the Sound.

13

Right: The awe-inspiring leap of the Sutherland Falls, which fall from Lake Quill in the vicinity of Milford Sound. The highest waterfall in New Zealand, it is much photographed by travellers walking the renowned Milford Track.

Far right: Doubtful Sound, named in 1770 by Captain Cook, who wanted to enter it but was afraid he might have to wait a long time for a favourable wind before he could leave. Parts of it were explored and renamed by Spanish explorer Don Alessandro Malaspina in 1793.

One of the most dominant features of the park is Milford Sound which was named by Captain John Grono after Milford Haven in his native Wales. In the Sound, perhaps aboard a cautiously exploring cruise ship or a more manoeuvrable tourist launch, it can be difficult to judge the true size of your surroundings.

The Sound really is 2.4km (1½ miles) across and those "hills" on either side are really 1524m (5000ft) high.

Mitre Peak spears upward for 1695m (5560ft) to become one of the world's highest mountains rising directly from the sea.

Lake Quill, a few kilometres away, is like a basin in the sky. The Sutherland Falls leap over a notch on its lip to plummet 580m (1904ft) to the valley below — the fourth highest waterfall in the world.

Right: Lake Te Anau, largest of the Southern lakes. A large and beautiful glowworm cave, known to the Maori of old, but not re-discovered until 1948, is a favourite tourist attraction.

Below, left to right: The kiwi, New Zealand's national symbol. Flightless, semi-nocturnal, and with feathers that are loose, shaggy and somewhat hair-like, the kiwi lays one of the largest eggs on earth proportionate to its body size.

The rare takahe (*Notornis mantelli*) was thought extinct until 1948, when a scientific party re-discovered it in a remote mountain valley in Fiordland.

The unique tuatara (*Sphenodon punctatus*) is the only living representative of the Mesozoic age. It has no relatives among other living reptiles, and is found only on 20 off-shore islands of New Zealand.

Typical New Zealand rain forest with vivid orange bracket fungus.

Right: **Lake Manapouri. Its original name, Moturau, meant "lake of a hundred islands", though in fact it was closer to thirty.**

Overleaf: **Lake Wanaka occupies an old glacier bed and is one of the source lakes for the mighty Clutha River. It reaches depths of more than 300m (1000ft).**

New Zealand is rich in lakes, each with its own character. Those in the South Island share a common glacial heritage. They tend to be long, narrow and winding, cold, and extremely deep.

The best known southern lakes are Te Anau, Manapouri, Wanaka, and Wakatipu. Most abound in fish. While the salmon, at nearly three kilos (6lbs), are smaller than northern hemisphere visitors might be used to, the fat brown and rainbow trout more than make up for them.

Te Anau is the largest lake in the South Island. It is 53km (33 miles) long, nearly ten kilometres (six miles) wide and up to 276m (906ft) deep. Te Anau has so many branches that some people suggest its name means "wanderer". Others, however, maintain that it means "cave of swirling waters".

Te Anau is particularly famous for its glow worm caves discovered in 1948. In these caves, the limestone is still "working" — water drips constantly down so that the strange shapes are still forming.

Lake Manapouri, 19km (12 miles) by road from Te Anau, is the centre of a massive hydro-electricity project which has caused fears that New Zealand could lose its most beautiful lake. Manapouri, the lake of the Sorrowing Heart, is New Zealand's deepest — 440m (1445ft) — and is dotted by 36 islands.

The small township of Wanaka on the shore of the lake of the same name increases its population of 900 tenfold during the holiday season. The lake is 305m (1000ft) deep and very cold, but offers excellent trout and salmon fishing.

For the visitor, Queenstown is a jumping-off place for many intriguing excursions by air, land, water, or on snow.

The town is linked with a comprehensive transport system covering the major tourist attractions in that part of the South Island and makes an excellent base for exploring the countryside.

There are the 293km^2 (113 square miles) of Lake Wakatipu, overlooked by the dramatic peaks of the Remarkables. The lake offers excellent fishing and a beautiful setting for launch outings.

Skiers head for Coronet Peak only 19km (12 miles) from Queenstown; railway enthusiasts board the Kingston Flyer, a restored steam train which makes regular trips between Kingston and Lumsden; other visitors go sightseeing on horseback, visit the Deer Haven Game Farm, inspect relics of mining days including Golden Terminal — a clever replica of a mining town — and the Centennial Museum at the genuine old mining village of Arrowtown.

After all this exertion there are many quiet walks to enjoy, or perhaps a meal at the Skyline Chalet 466m (1530ft) above Queenstown, reached by gondola cars on an aerial cableway.

Far left: **Steam buffs rejoice: the Kingston Flyer, a splendid steam locomotive, carries passengers between Kingston and Lumsden.**

Left: **Cardrona: a wild gold mining town in the 1860s, now rich only in memories.**

Below and overleaf: **The Golden Terminal, a reconstructed gold mining town near Queenstown.**

The main street of Queenstown, looking across Lake
Wakatipu.

Far right: Tasman Glacier.

Right: The razor-like ridge along the triple peak of Mt Cook, known to the Maori as Aorangi, the Cloud Piercer.

Below: Landing on the Tasman Glacier in a skiplane, Mt Cook National Park. The largest glacier in the Southern Alps, the Tasman is over 3km (2 miles) wide at its widest point.

Overleaf: Sunset on Mt Cook. First climbed on December 24, 1894, the mountain is today a popular challenge for experienced climbers.

Mt Cook National Park offers visitors to New Zealand some of the greatest excitement they will ever experience. For many people this comes in the form of skiplane flights around the mountain peaks, climaxed by a landing on the mighty Tasman Glacier.

The Maoris gave Mt Cook the name Aorangi, which means Cloud Piercer, and this, New Zealand's highest mountain, is well worth the trip alone.

First class accommodation is provided at The Hermitage, tucked away at the foot of the mountains.

Westland National Park is on the opposite side of the Southern Alps to Mt Cook, but still offers plenty of alpine scenery, including the two massive glaciers, the Franz Josef and the Fox.

As well, there are fine lakes, wild and deserted beaches, towns steeped in history and still with an air of frontier times about them, and the lush confusion of temperate rain forests. There is much to see in the park's 88,608ha (218,956 acres) and travellers are advised to avail themselves of the many highly-detailed tourist brochures.

Far left: **This scene is typical of the unexpected juxtaposition of alpine scenery and temperate rain forest encountered in Westland. Mt Bismarck, Westland National Park.**

Above: Glaciated rock, Franz Josef Glacier.

Left: Franz Josef Glacier, Westland. 12 km (8 miles) long, it descends on a gradient of about 1000 m per 3 km (1000 ft per mile)

Left: **Glacial moraine, Franz Josef Glacier.**

Above: **Punakaiki (Pancake) Rocks, between Greymouth and Westport, are composed of weathered stratified limestone. Complete with blowholes and subterranean chasms, Punakaiki can be an unforgettable spectacle.**

35

Right: Inside the shearing shed, a weary worker takes time out for a break. New Zealand holds third place in the world as a producer of wool, and second place as an exporter.

Below: Farm workers round cattle into trucks, Haast district. New Zealanders have the world's highest meat consumption per capita.

Apart from comparatively brief flurries with gold, timber and kauri gum, sheep and cattle have always been the mainstay of New Zealand's economy.

In fact, sheep outnumber humans better than 19 to 1. At the last count, New Zealand had about 56,400,000 sheep, 6,505,000 beef cattle, 2,990,000 dairy cattle and, to keep alive the New Zealand tradition of Christmas hams, 536,000 pigs.

In spite of great progress in other areas, New Zealand's major export earners are meat, wool, and dairy products.

New Zealanders have made a science out of raising grass. This has allowed stock loadings on pastures that amaze many visiting farmers.

Overleaf: **Golden sun over Canterbury's golden fleece.**

And sheep farmers prove the old saying about dogs being man's best friend. One shepherd with his dogs can control an incredible number of sheep using a series of whistles which established communication between them that verges on the telepathic.

The shearing photograph on this page was taken on a farm on the Canterbury Plains near Christchurch. At the 1977 world shearing championships in Great Britain, a New Zealander took first place, an expatriate New Zealander competing for Austria was second, an Australian — how did he get in here? — was third, and yet another New Zealander was fourth. And yes, there are women shearers. Lots of them.

Bluff, New Zealand's southernmost port of any consequence, has a special place in the hearts — or rather the stomachs — of gourmets. It is the home port for the fishing boats that gather the famed Bluff oysters.

In later years, it has also become the base for an aluminium smelting plant which draws its power from the much-criticised Manapouri power project.

Left: **Famous Bluff oysters are swiftly opened at the hands of an expert.**

Below: **Shearers on a farm on the Canterbury Plains near Christchurch.**

A young country, shaped and pulled by titanic forces. Ripples in the earth's crust form these tussocky hills between Queenstown and Benmore.

Barely 27km (17 miles) away is Invercargill, the principal city of Southland Province and the centre of a fertile farming area. It is also the southern terminus of the main trunk railway line and the national airline, Air New Zealand.

Further north on the east coast is the major port city of Dunedin, one of New Zealand's four main population centres.

The drive up the coast to the "waist" of the South Island is pleasant and brings you to Christchurch, the South Island's largest city and the centre of a new range of experiences.

Above: The Moeraki Boulders formed as secretions in the nearby cliff, some 60 million years ago, and have been eroded by wave action. Weighing several tons, the largest is almost 4 metres in circumference.

This broad, man- made
lake was formed by
the giant earth dam of the
Benmore Power Project.

After the upward-reaching peaks of Fiordland and the Southern Alps, the sprawling Canterbury Plains with their braided river beds and geometric arrangements of fields stretching to the horizon, provide a true contrast of opposites.

Settled gracefully in the centre, gathering its suburban skirts around it in queenly fashion, is Christchurch. The placenames in the area underline many times the Englishness of the region. It is as though the pioneers sought to rebuke the temerity of the French who tried to claim sovereignty of the South Island at Akaroa, 84km (52 miles) to the South-east.

After drinking your fill of Christchurch's peaceful atmosphere and admiring the river Avon and spectacular parks, a visit to Akaroa where the French influence has been preserved is well worth while.

From Christchurch, visitors can depart to Australia via the international airport or drive north to Picton and the sunken valleys of the Marlborough Sounds where they can catch vehicular ferries to Wellington. If your itinerary allows it, a visit to the Sounds will be a memorable experience.

The two main sounds at Marlborough are Pelorus and Queen Charlotte, but there are numerous islands and small inlets in a setting that contains enough twists and surprises to delight anyone.

Some of the first contacts between Maoris and Europeans took place around the northern bays of the South Island and it is therefore natural that the area is rich in history.

Fishermen delight in the clear, blue waters which offer a generous variety of catch, particularly blue cod, gurnard, and groper.

Top left: **View of the Avon River at Christchurch showing the "iron lace" which decorates many of the bridges.**

Bottom left: **Cashel Street near Bridge of Remembrance, Christchurch.**

Below left: **The Christchurch Town Hall: a cultural complex of auditoria with restaurant and exhibition facilities.**

Far left: **The sprawl of Christchurch: its neatly-gridded streets containing neatly-manicured gardens.**

Left: **Nelson's leafy parks and gardens are a summer delight.**

Below: **Mailboxes stand silent sentinel over Moenui Bay, near Picton, Marlborough Sounds.**

Overleaf: **The long arms of the Marlborough Sounds as seen from the air. If driving through New Zealand you will enter one of these sounds on the ferry when crossing from the North Island. It's an entertaining day trip from Wellington, too, in the summer.**

The main centres of population are Nelson, Blenheim and Picton. As the district enjoys one of the highest sunshine averages in New Zealand, it has become known for its fruit, hops, tobacco, vegetables, and in recent years its grapes and wine. In Nelson is found a monument marking the geographical centre of New Zealand.

Picton, on the eastern arm of Queen Charlotte Sound, is the northern terminal of the South Island's main trunk railway line, but bridges Cook Strait with vehicular and rail ferries to Wellington.

49

North Island

Russell
Great Barrier Island
Auckland
Hamilton
•Rotorua
•Taupo
New Plymouth
▲Mt. Egmont
Napier
•Wanganui
Palmerston North
Wellington

Right: **Mt Egmont,** at 2518m the North Island's second highest peak.

HAVING INSPECTED Maui's canoe, we turn to Te Ika a Maui, the fish of Maui, or the North Island. And if Maui had the same weaknesses as his modern brothers of the hook and line in any country, he probably never stopped talking about this catch.

But why should he? In its own way, the North Island is just as mystical, appealing, intriguing as the South Island.

It has by far the greater population and concentration of industry, yet retains its remote and wild places that sometimes claim the lives of inexperienced or careless trampers and climbers.

The North Island has the greater Maori population and this adds a special richness where the two cultures complement each other in a way that is special to New Zealand.

And, getting back to fishy stories, Maui's catch has plenty of life in it yet. The central volcanic plateau has been harnessed to provide geothermal power and not far from the awesome crater left by the Tarawera eruption last century, Mt Ngauruhoe smoulders away.

Wellington, the nation's capital, is said to have the cleanest air in New Zealand — because it never stays in one place long enough to get dirty! But, while it's true that the funnel of the surrounding hills can produce gale-force winds, the hills also frame a harbour rated among the most beautiful in the world.

The Cenotaph and
its equestrian statue
remember New Zealand's
dead in several wars; but
the living put up monu-
ments to commerce — as
the flourishing office
blocks (rear) testify.

The capital has all the dignity its station could require, and few people who have lived there can avoid the occasional sudden pang of nostalgia, a legacy of good times with good people.

One of the most pleasant ways to take in much of Wellington and the neighbouring Hutt Valley at once is to climb or drive to the top of the same hills that enclose the settled areas. Particularly rewarding are the views from Mt Victoria and from the top of the cable car which ascends from the downtown area to Kelburn.

Above: A glimpse of suburban Wellington with a view towards the satellite cities of Upper Hutt and Lower Hutt (right, distance). Visitors often boggle at the brightly-coloured boxes, clinging to steep hillsides, which house the capital's inhabitants.

Lambton Quay, Wellington. Shortage of flat land in downtown Wellington — much of today's commercial area is reclaimed from the sea — means high-rise office buildings abound in the capital city.

Top: Three varieties of palm tree are reflected in this pool in a Napier Park.

Centre: The Square is the main feature of Palmerston North, a university town.

Bottom: Beautiful Puke-kura Park, New Plymouth, is the perfect place from which to view Mt Egmont.

Far right: Wanganui, on the river of the same name. Trips by jet boat to the scenic upper reaches of the river have become a tourist "must".

In spite of the arrival of television in the early 1960s, New Zealanders are still an active people, whether they are vigorously pursuing the arts or sport.

But, at the risk of offending the art lovers, it would be fair to say that sport has a special hold on a country the bulk of whose population is still teenaged.

While the achievements in the arts and in sport have been out of all proportion for a small country, sport as a topic for discussion can be fraught with as many perils for the unwary as politics and religion!

Left: Watersports are popular in a country well-endowed with lakes, rivers and sea coast.

Below: Horse-racing — New Zealand's favourite pastime. Many world-famous racehorses are bred from renowned New Zealand bloodstock lines.

The national rugby representatives, known as the All Blacks.

Far left: The meeting house was — and is — the heartbeat of Maori tribal life. Here, and on the marae in front of it, the important discussions and ceremonies took place.

Left: In historic times, Maori songs and chants used a subtle musical scale very strange to the European ear, comprising only a few tones. Today, however, the melodies they compose on the more familiar European style are a delight.

Overleaf: These former spa buildings now house the museum, Rotorua. The important collection of Maori artefacts and intriguing early photos of the region merit a visit — and it's still possible to "take the waters" nearby.

The National Museum in Wellington and the Auckland War Memorial Museum contain probably the finest collections of Polynesian artefacts in the world.

However, in New Zealand's countryside there are many evidences that for the Maori people their culture is not to be confined to buildings that remember the past. It is alive and vivid. What is more, many pakehas (Europeans) have made it clear that they want to share it too.

Both racial groupings have much to offer each other and will continue to prosper so long as they remember that they need each other.

While it is true that before the coming of the Europeans, Maoris did not use metal tools or have a written language in the accepted sense, they were in other ways a highly skilled and cultured people.

There is currently a resurgence of interest in the Maori arts, crafts and culture.

Far left: From the earliest days of tourism, visitors have been enchanted by bright-eyed local children "diving for pennies" from the Whakarewarewa bridge into the warm stream beneath. Today the junior aquanauts are as busy as ever — but inflation has left pennies far behind! These children are enjoying the backyard hot pools found in many homes in the thermal area.

Left: Gottfried Lindauer, a Bohemian artist who took up residence in New Zealand in 1873, painted many of the notable Maori leaders of his day. His detailed paintings faithfully record what was even then a fast-vanishing way of life. Lindauer's paintings may be seen in the Auckland City Art Gallery, and the New Plymouth and Wanganui Museums. Represented here is Haora Tipa Koinaki, a rangatira (chief) and warrior of the Thames district, later in the 1860s a peacemaker.

On 10 June, 1886, people living near Mt Tarawera in the Rotorua district thought the world had ended — and indeed for 153 of them it had.

The supposedly extinct volcano erupted in horrific fashion for six hours. Its fury killed 147 Maoris, six Europeans, destroyed three villages, dried up a 115ha (284-acre) lake, shattered roads and bridges, coated 15,540km^2 (6000 square miles) of forest and farmland with ash, and obliterated one of the modern wonders of the world — the fabled Pink and White Terraces.

As the stunned survivors groped their way to safety, many became lost in the totally alien landscape that a few hours before had been home ground.

Today all but the most grievous scars have been healed by nature, but it is easy to be stunned into awed silence as you scud over the craters that still testify to the inferno.

Not all the examples of volcanic activity in the area are as grim. There is something inescapably humorous about the rude bloic! bloic! of boiling mud. The graceful Pohutu Geyser and its many smaller counterparts make fine colour photographs. So too do the chemical rainbows that streak the earth.

Even the ground-shaking fury of the thermal power bores at Wairakei near Taupo are reassuringly under control as they transform their primitive force into understandable electricity.

Further south, scientists keep a close watch on smoking Mt Ngauruhoe and thousands ski daily on twin-peaked Mt Ruapehu, with its hot crater lake.

Far left: **The best skiing mountain in the North Island . . . and it's a volcano! Rope tow, Mt Ruapehu.**

Left: **Chemical rainbows caused by volcanic activity, Waiotapu, Rotorua district.**

Right: Pohutu Geyser plays daily at Whakarewarewa, Rotorua.

Below: **Colours at Waimangu. A black-water geyser once erupted 500 metres (1500ft) into the air at this site.**

Far right: **Anglers the world over flock to New Zealand lakes and rivers for the finest in fishing. They say if you've never eaten fresh trout, you haven't tasted trout at all.**

At Whakarewarewa Village in Rotorua, tourists can wander through a bubbling, boiling, hissing, spurting wonderland and see how the Maori people learned to live with the thermal activity. The Rotorua experience is one not to be missed.

Rotorua is within easy driving distance of Auckland, but there is so much to divert travellers along the way that those with plenty of time could easily take several days to complete the 234km direct route.

However, Rotorua is an ideal jumping-off point for an almost unlimited range of activities. To the south there is Lake Taupo, a virtual inland sea. It has a world-wide reputation as a trout fishing centre.

Three volcanoes nestle cheek-by-jowl in the centre of the North Island. Ngauruhoe is at the right and Ruapehu to the rear in this shot of Tongariro National Park.

Further south again is Tongariro National Park where Mts Tongariro, Ruapehu, and Ngauruhoe hold sway. Due directly west is Taranaki Province with the near perfect cone of Mt Egmont.

To the north of Rotorua on the east coast are the twin port and beach resort centres of Tauranga and Mt Maunganui. Westward from these, near the centre of the narrowing island is Hamilton, the hub of the rich Waikato farming district.

Right: **Thousands of visitors to the Waitomo Caves, south of Hamilton, travel on an underground river to see this magical sight. The New Zealand glow-worm lets down as many as seventy "fishing lines" to catch its dinner — the tiny flying insects that inhabit the caves and grottos in which it lives.**

Far right: **Bridal Veil Falls, near Raglan. Waterfalls are among the country's most photogenic scenery.**

Overleaf: **Piha, one of the most popular surfing beaches within easy reach of Auckland, is dominated by Lion Rock.**

Left: Another surfing area and popular holiday resort is Mt Maunganui in the Bay of Plenty. Traces of ancient Maori fortifications are still to be seen on the mount itself.

Above: Whether a passionate fisherman or simply one who likes "messing about in boats", you will enjoy the intimate scenery and uncluttered waters of the beautiful Bay of Islands.

In former times
a gold-rush area, Coro-
mandel Harbour today
sees a summer boom in
tourists.

The huge kauri
Tane Mahuta is easily seen
in Waipoua Forest. Many
of the ancient forest giants
are over 2000 years old,
and their felling is rigidly
controlled by Act of
Parliament.

Above: **The pohutukawa tree** (*Metrosideros excelsa*) **blazes in crimson glory from late December through January. Early settlers in this country named it the Christmas tree.**

Left: **The astonishing stick insect, of which New Zealand has numerous species. To the ancient Maori, the sex of a future child was indicated by which of two sorts of stick insect alighted on a pregnant woman.**

85

Hamilton straddles the majestic Waikato River which in its run to the sea is used many times over as a source of hydro-electric power.

Auckland sprawls 127km directly to the north, occupying all of the narrow neck of land separating its two main harbours, the Waitemata and the Manukau.

Auckland is a world in itself. At first it may seem like "just another big city", but on closer examination its unique Pacific character becomes evident.

Because of its close links with the sea it has become the sail-boat building and yachting capital of New Zealand. Its eastern skyline is dominated by the island of Rangitoto which blasted its way out of the ocean some 750 years ago.

Launch and floatplane excursions leave daily to the many beautiful islands in the Hauraki Gulf Maritime Park and "flightseeing" as far north as the historic and breathtaking Bay of Islands is popular with visitors.

Further across the Gulf are two of Aucklanders' most popular holiday areas — the once gold-rich Coromandel Peninsula and off its tip, Great Barrier Island.

Far left: **Auckland by night.**

Left: **Auckland Harbour Bridge.**

Overleaf: **Auckland seen from the top of Mt Victoria, on the North Shore. Devonport is in the foreground, with the Naval Base at the far right.**

Right: Cape Reinga, at the top of the North Island. In Maori lore, the souls of the departed approach here down the face of a steep cliff to a pohutu-kawa tree, where they leap off to the spirit world.

In exploring the country north of Auckland, many visitors take advantage of organised coach tours because there is so much to see. Lovers of history and big game fishing can visit the Bay of Islands and those who thrill to legends can stand on lonely Cape Reinga on New Zealand's northernmost tip where the spirits of the Maori dead are said to leap off on their homeward journey to Hawaiiki, the land of their fathers.

Wherever you go, whatever you do, your New Zealand holiday is something you will never forget.

Appendix A-Z

ACCOMMODATION: There are privately-owned hotels and motels in all main centres. Tourist Hotel Corporation hotels have been established by the Government in remoter tourist areas. Motor camping is popular. The usual arrangement is for campers to provide their own tents or caravans (trailers) and the camp to provide community washing, cooking and toilet facilities. Some camping grounds also have cabins. Hotels range from international class to small private bed-and-breakfast establishments. The Tourist and Publicity Department has prepared an inventory of accommodation.

AERO CLUBS: Most of the main centres have aero clubs and it is often possible to arrange charters or sightseeing flights through them.

AERODROMES: New Zealand has 54 aerodromes with public licences, 67 licensed private aerodromes, 197 authorised landing places, and 22 government civil aerodromes.

ARROWTOWN: A historic mining town 13 miles north-east of Queenstown. Swimming, fishing, tramping, mountain climbing and general sightseeing. Lakes District Centennial Museum has many relics of mining days. Visitors can pan for gold in Arrow River.

AUCKLAND: Largest metropolitan, commercial and industrial centre in New Zealand. It is a principal port of call for international and coastal shipping and has a major international airport and internal airways terminal. There are rail and bus links to all parts of the North Island. Major motorway construction serves the third highest traffic-population ratio in the world. There are many parks and reserves, fine bathing beaches, bush walks, theatres, restaurants and nightspots. The Auckland Central Public Library contains an excellent collection of rare books. The Auckland City Art Gallery is rated as one of the two best in the southern hemisphere. Another important cultural asset is the Auckland Institute and Museum which houses one of the world's finest collection of Pacific artifacts. At Western Springs is the Museum of Transport and Technology which is very popular with families on its ''live'' weekends when many of the vintage vehicles and machines are operating. An eight-lane Harbour Bridge links the central City area with the North Shore and main highway north.

BAY OF ISLANDS: The site of the earliest permanent settlement of Europeans and one of the most beautiful and interesting parts of the country. The Treaty of Waitangi which ended hostilities between Maoris and Europeans was signed there on February 6, 1840. The area contains about 800km (500 miles) of irregular coastline and 149 islands. It was made famous as a big game fishing area by American writer, Zane Grey.

BIG GAME FISHING: Many world record catches have been caught in New Zealand waters — the principal game fishing areas being Whangaroa, Russell, (Bay of Islands), Whitianga (Mercury Bay), Whakatane and Tauranga. Specially-equipped launches with trained crews may be hired. Catches include striped marlin, black marlin, blue marlin, broadbill, mako shark, hammerhead shark, tiger shark, thresher shark, kingfish (yellow tail) and tuna. Best season, February, but fishing good from December — April.

BLENHEIM: Pleasant holiday town near Marlborough Sounds at the northern tip of the South Island. Enjoys the highest quota of sunshine hours in New Zealand.

CAPE BRETT: Popular Big Game Fishing area in the Bay of Islands.

CAPE KIDNAPPERS: A gannet rookery at Hawke Bay reputed to be the only mainland gannetry known. Visitors must obtain a permit from the Commissioner of Crown Lands in Napier, or from Clifton Domain office before entering the sanctuary. The best time to visit is between November and December when the birds are nesting.

CAPE REINGA: At the northern tip of New Zealand; visited by coach tours. According to legend it is here that the souls of the Maori dead depart for their final resting place.

CANTERBURY PLAIN: Situated in the central area of the South

Island between the Pacific (eastern) coast and the Southern Alps. About 193 km (120 miles) long and no more than 64km (40 miles) wide. Mostly river flats.

CECIL PEAK: A mountain on the western shores of Lake Wakatipu near Queenstown. Cecil Peak Station, a popular calling point for sightseers, is becoming an important tourist attraction.

CHATEAU TONGARIRO: Tourist ski resort in Tongariro National Park, central North Island. First-class hotel, cabins, tennis courts and nine-hole golf course.

CHRISTCHURCH: The major city of the South Island. Served by the Port of Lyttelton and situated on the east coast near the "waist" of the island. It has an international airport and is a major road and rail centre. Has a distinct English atmosphere accentuated by Cathedral Square, the focal point of the commercial area, the beautiful River Avon, fine parks and English street and place names. An easy drive from Christchurch is Akaroa Bay where the French attempted to claim sovereignty of the South Island The Centennial Hall at the Canterbury Museum has a particularly well-executed reconstruction of pioneer times. The new Town Hall also merits a visit.

CHURCHES: See Religion

CLIMATE: New Zealand has a temperate climate with little real difference between summer and winter months. In Northland and western districts of both islands, the annual range is about 8°C. For the remainder of the North Island and east coast districts of the South Island it is 9° − 10°C. In some inland places, the variation can be as much as 11°C and in Central Otago, which approaches a more Continental type of climate, the range can be 14°C. Generally, mean temperatures at sea level in the north are about 15°C and decrease steadily southward to 12°C in the Cook Strait area to 9°C in the deep south. Rainfall is generous and the greater variation is east-west because of the mountain ranges that divide the country. While the extremes are as little as 300mm annually in a pocket of Central Otago and 7000mm in the Southern Alps, most areas would fall between the range 600mm and 1500mm. Areas exposed to the west and southwest experience much showery weather with rain falling on half the days of the year. Snow rarely falls below the 600m mark in mountainous areas, even in winter. In inland Canterbury and Otago, though, where there are grazing areas about 300m, snowfalls have caused serious stock losses in the more severe winters. In both islands sheep and cattle remain in the open all year round. Humidity is usually between 70 and 80 per cent in coastal areas and about 10 per cent lower inland. Humidity varies according to the temperature, falling to a minimum during the afternoon when the temperature is at its highest and often rising to between 90 and 100 per cent on clear nights.

CLUTHA RIVER: The largest river in New Zealand. It is in the South Island and has as its main sources the lakes Hawea, Wanaka and Wakatipu. Most of the tributary streams are gold-bearing and much wealth was won from the area in early days. The river was originally named the Molyneux, by Captain Cook, but the name "Clutha" which had been in general use, was made official in 1952.

COOK, Captain James (1728-1779): A great English navigator and explorer who, in 1769, made the first charts of New Zealand while returning home from observing the transit of Venus from Tahiti. Returned twice to continue his explorations, but was killed by natives at Hawaii during his third voyage.

COOK STRAIT: The passage between the North and South Islands. Discovered by and named after Captain James Cook. The strait, often turbulent, is 18km (11 miles) wide at its narrowest point and has been swum in modern times in spite of difficult currents. Rail and vehicular ferries cross daily between Wellington and Picton.

COROMANDEL PENINSULA: A rugged, but extremely scenic peninsula in the North Island. Known for forestry and gold mining in the past; now enjoying growing importance as a tourist and holiday centre. Site of 63,942ha (158,000-acre) forest park.

CORONET PEAK: Ski-field near Queenstown, one of the South Island's main tourist regions. The best powder snow in New Zealand, on a developed field, is to be found there.

CRAYFISH: New Zealand rock lobster. Caught for local consumption, but most is exported — particularly to the United States of America.

CURRENCY: In 1967, New Zealand changed to decimal currency from a pounds, shillings, and pence system. The present dollar is the equivalent of the old 10-shilling note and the 10c coin replaces the former shilling. Notes are now in issue for 1, 2, 5, 10, 20 and 100 dollars. While a $1 coin has been struck, it is not in general issue. Coins circulating include cupronickel 50c, 20c, 10c, and 5c pieces. The lc and 2c coins are of bronze.

DAIRY FARMING: One of New Zealand's key industries. Farm products and pulp, paper, and paperboard account for about 80 per cent of the total value of merchandise exports. In 1975 meat products earned about $430 million, dairy products $290 million, and wool $260 million.

DEER FARMING: Assuming growing importance as venison finds a ready overseas market. However, deer farming is strictly controlled by the Department of Agriculture because of the status of wild deer as noxious animals.

DOUBTFUL SOUND: In Fiordland National Park — a large sound with many branches, one of which leads to Deep Cove, base camp for the Manapouri power project. Deep Cove is now accessible by a road which has made possible a drive which has become a scenic highlight of any visit to the area. The sound has several fine waterfalls.

DUNEDIN: The second largest city in the South Island, a university city and busy commercial and industrial port. Has many fine walks, gardens and reserves. Dunedin's history dates from the arrival of the ships *John Wickliffe* on March 23, 1848 and the *Phillip Laing* on April 15. It was first intended to call the settlement New Edinburgh, but instead it was given Edinburgh's more ancient name (Dun Edin — Edin on the Hill). Almost immediately it assumed a cultural and commercial importance which lasts to this day.

EARTHQUAKES: Seismic activity in New Zealand can be compared roughly with that of California. A shock of Richter magnitude 6 or above occurs on the average of about once a year. A magnitude 7 quake is expected once in 10 years and one of about magnitude 8 probably once a century. The greatest seismic disaster recorded was the Napier earthquake of 1931 which claimed 255 lives and the Buller earthquake of 1929 in which there were 17 people killed. The total death toll from all other shocks since 1840 is less than 15. New Zealand's seismological observatory is in Wellington.

ELECTRICITY: The bulk of New Zealand's electricity is generated by harnessing the water in lakes and rivers, the most-used river being the Waikato which flows through Lake Taupo in the North Island to Port Waikato on the west coast just south of Auckland. The gold mining boom town of Reefton in the South Island had electric power as early as 1888 and Wellington followed the next year using water power from the city mains, but later switched to steam. Today at Wairakei near Lake Taupo, natural steam is used to drive the turbines; coal is used at the Meremere steam station south of Auckland; an oil-fired steam station has operated at Marsden Point near Whangarei since 1967; gas turbines have been generating power at Otahuhu in South Auckland since 1968; a large station has been built at New Plymouth to use either oil or part of the off-shore reserves of natural gas; and a large gas and coal-fired station is being built at Huntly. Considerable controversy surrounds the suggestion that nuclear power plants may be opened early next century. Until then, most North Island stations are expected to use natural gas, oil, or coal. Power cables under the waters of Cook Strait link the North and South Islands.

ETHNIC GROUPS: About 85 per cent of those enumerated in the 1971 census gave New Zealand as their place of birth. Others listed the United Kingdom (8.7 per cent), Australia (1.5 per cent), Pacific Islands (1.1 per cent), the Netherlands (0.7 per cent), Ireland (0.3 per cent), India (0.2 per cent), and China (0.1 per cent).

EXPORTS: Farm products and pulp, paper, and paperboard account for about 80 per cent of the total value of New Zealand's merchandise exports. In 1975, meat products earned about $430 million, dairy products $290 million, and wool $260 million. The traditional market for the bulk of New Zealand's export butter and cheese, wool, and meat products is the United Kingdom. However, access to this market became less certain when Britain joined the European Economic Community. New Zealand has since turned its attention elsewhere, establishing new markets and developing existing trading relationships. Major trading partners now include Australia, Japan, the United States of America, with growing ties in South America and the Middle East. Manufacturing industries are enjoying a growing importance, but the economy is still geared to the success of the country's agricultural exports. Indeed, New Zealand is more dependent than most countries upon trade. For example, in spite of its smallness, New Zealand holds third place in the world as a producer of wool and second place as an exporter. Most of the wool is from crossbred sheep. Generally, New Zealand is a producer of high quality foods at relatively low cost. Another important "export" is the expertise acquired in the process.

FISHING — freshwater: New Zealand has a world-wide reputation for its trout fishing. Rainbow and brown trout abound in the lakes and rivers of both main islands along with quinnat salmon and perch in the south. The main trout fishing areas in the North Island are around the Rotorua lakes and Taupo. Licences are necessary, but a chat with the staff of a local sports store will give you all the information you require. In the South Island, lake systems in main tourist areas provide excellent fishing. Sea-run brown trout average 2.3kg (5lb) in West Coast rivers and sea-run quinnat salmon about 5.5kg (12lb) in East Coast rivers.

FORESTS: When the first settlers came to New Zealand, extensive evergreen forests covered some two-thirds of the country. Today about a quarter of the total land area is in forests, much of it retained in parks and remoter areas for soil protection and water regulation. Apart from national parks, about 4 million hectares of land has been constituted State forest, valuable either for timber or conservation purposes.

GEMSTONES: New Zealand has a range of gemstones wide enough to keep most rockhounds happy. Pride of place goes to greenstone, sometimes called New Zealand jade. Greenstone is found as

Bowenite or the harder and more valuable Nephrite which was used by early Maoris for weapons, tools and jewellery. The best known source of Bowenite is Anita Bay in Fiordland. Nephrite is still found in the rivers of Westland where it was first won by parties of foraging Maoris and later by the dredges of the Europeans. However, to have much chance of success today, rock-hounds generally have to move into the headwaters where the dredges could not go. In 1976, a bulldozer was used at a Westland Bay to haul in a huge off-shore boulder which proved to be a $100,000 lump of greenstone. Another boulder, measuring more than 2 metres by 1 metre (7ft by 4ft) was found by a helicopter pilot in a remote part of Mt Aspiring National Park and estimated to weigh 25 tons. Greenstone actually ranges in colour from milky-white to almost black and is hard to recognise in the raw state. Other semi-precious stones found in New Zealand are listed in the fine Reed book, *Gemstones of New Zealand,* by Lyn and Ray Cooper.

Their list includes: Agate, amethyst, amethyst quartz, aventurine, bloodstone, bowenite, carnelian, chalcedony, citrine, chert, cherty flint, flint, garnet, jasper, milky quartz, nephrite, obsidian, onyx, opal-common, opal-precious (extremely rare), orthoclane feldspar, petrified wood, quartz crystal or rock crystal, quartzite, rhodonite, rose quartz, rhyolite, sard, schists, serpentine.

GLACIERS: In the South Island there is a considerable glacial system. The largest glacier is the Tasman near Mt. Cook. The Tasman is visited by ski-planes which land at selected points on its 29km by 9km expanse. As with other glaciers on the eastern slopes of the alps, its rate of flow is slow and its terminal face is above 600m. Other important glaciers on the eastern slopes are the Murchison (17km), Mueller (13km), Godley (13km), and Hooker (11km). Heavier snow-falls on the western slopes make glaciers more numerous and allow them to descend to lower levels. The steeper slopes give them a more rapid rate of flow. The two best known are the Fox and the Franz Josef with lengths of 15km and 13km respectively. Their terminal faces are at 200m and 210m.

GOVERNMENT: The Queen of England is the Queen of New Zealand as well. She is represented in this country by a governor-general appointed for a five-year term, but the task of government falls to a 92-member House of Representatives. The country has been divided into 88 general electorates where New Zealanders of any race can stand for election, and four seats reserved for Maoris. In the last century, New Zealand was one of the pioneers in giving women the vote. Today, with few exceptions, any citizen aged 18 or over is entitled to vote. Since the Second World War, the political scene has been dominated by the National Party (Conservatives) with its main rival being the Labour Party (Socialist). Members of parliament are elected for three-year terms and the party which captures most of the seats (rather than the majority of votes) becomes the government. The parliamentary leader of the ruling party becomes the Prime Minister and selects a cabinet of ministers to head the various portfolios. It has proved extremely difficult for an independent candidate to be elected to parliament and of the two most important minority parties, Social Credit and Values, only the former had ever held a seat up to late 1978.

GREAT BARRIER ISLAND: The largest of the North Island's off-shore islands, ranked fourth in the New Zealand group behind South, North, and Stewart islands. It is situated off the tip of the Coromandel Peninsula about 90km (56 miles) north-east of Auckland. It is about 40km (25 miles) long and 16km (10 miles) wide and can be reached by seaplane and conventional light aircraft (from Auckland) or by ferry. The rugged coastline has claimed several ships.

HANGI: Maori earth oven, also known as an umu, kopa, or hapi. A 30cm (12in) to 50cm (18in) pit is dug and filled with dry fuel above the ground level. Flat river stones are placed on top of the material and the fire ignited. The stones are allowed to get very hot — if necessary extra fuel can be placed over them as the fire is burning. When the fire has burned down, unburned sticks or large embers are removed. Some of the stones are taken out to place on top of the food. A generous layer of green leaves or ferns is placed over the remaining stones at the bottom of the pit and the food to be cooked is placed on top. The food is covered with more leaves after being sprinkled with a copious quantity of water. The last of the stones are placed in position and everything is buried under a good layer of earth which is tamped down to retain the steam. Cooking times vary according to the food item, with meat generally taking about two hours a pound, but as food cannot be spoiled by overcooking in a hangi, it's best to be in no hurry.

HAAST PASS: The lowest pass through the Southern Alps. It was opened for road traffic in 1965, thus making possible a spectacular round-the-island road journey. The pass connects the Haast River area in the west with the Makarora River in the east and reaches an altitude of 563m (1847 ft.)

HAMILTON: An important provincial centre situated on the Waikato River about 127km south of Auckland. Has strong historical links with the Maori people. Today it is a leading farming region and has a large number of smaller towns within its sphere of influence. A short distance outside the city proper is the community of Temple View which gets its name from being the location of the only Mormon temple in the Southern Hemisphere.

HAURAKI GULF MARITIME PARK: A 9500-hectare marine park administered from Auckland. It stretches northward to the Poor Knights Islands and has its southernmost point at the Alderman Islands on the eastern side of the Coromandel Peninsula. The park's territory encloses about 40 islands which include sanctuaries for bird or animal life either rare or found nowhere else in the world. Some of the islands are visited by regular ferry and amphibian services from Auckland, but it is necessary to obtain a permit from the Park Board to land on the sanctuary of Little Barrier Island.

KIWI: A nocturnal flightless bird unique to New Zealand and found in bush areas of both major islands. It has been adopted as a national symbol and New Zealanders are known the world over as "Kiwis". Dip into your pocket or purse for a 20 cent piece and study the likeness of the kiwi bird on its reverse side. Like the much larger, but now extinct moa, the kiwi belongs to the order *apterygiformes* which dates to the end of the earth's Cretaceous period 70 million years ago. Besides its age, there are several other peculiarities to the species. The kiwi stands about a foot high on short, powerful legs and has no tail, wings, or breastbone. Unlike most birds, the kiwi has a keen sense of smell. Its nostrils are situated at the end of its long, flexible beak which is used to forage for worms, grubs and insects. The egg laid by the female and incubated by the male weighs about 500 grams and is probably larger in proportion to body size than that of any other bird. Kiwis are usually brown or grey coloured with darker shadings or spots. The feathers are hair-like and were used to decorate the cloaks of Maori dignitaries. The kiwi is supposed to get its name from the kee-wee cry of the male.

LAKES: New Zealand's largest lakes in terms of area are: Taupo (North Island) 606 square kilometres, Te Anau (South Island) 344 square kilometres, Wakatipu (SI) 293, Wanaka (SI) 192, Ellesmere (SI) 181, Manapouri (SI) 142, Hawea (SI) 119, Tekapo (SI) 96, Pukaki (SI) 83, Rotorua (NI) 80, Wairarapa (NI) 80. The deepest lakes are: Manapouri (SI) 443 metres, Hawea (SI) 392, Wakatipu (SI) 378, Te Anau (SI) 276, Waikaremoana (NI) 256, Coleridge (SI) 207, Kaniere (SI) 197, Tekapo (SI) 189, Taupo (NI) 159. In addition there are more than a dozen sizeable artificial lakes associated with power projects.

MAORIS: The Polynesian natives of New Zealand. When the Europeans first came to New Zealand, the Maoris were living in tribal groupings in fortified villages known as pas. Today, although integration has taken place, land is still of vital importance to the

Maori people. The marae or common land of the home village assumes almost sacred proportions. Even in the cities where Maoris of many tribal groupings may live in a particular neighbourhood, there is currently a strong move toward the formation of urban maraes or community centres. Traditionally Northland, Auckland and the Waikato district are strong centres of Maori population. Visitors may see models of pas at most museums. At Whakare-warewa at Rotorua, a replica of a small village has been built and guides are on hand to explain village life and the purposes of the buildings to visitors. There is a similar village at Kerikeri in the Bay of Islands.

MAPS: The first Europeans to see many parts of New Zealand were intrepid mapmakers. Today their fine traditions of craftsman-ship and willingness to "go anywhere, do anything" in pursuit of knowledge, has been married to such modern technology as aerial mapping and satellite photography. The result is a particularly fine series of maps which can be obtained from Government Printing Office bookstores. Similarly, a wide range of atlases, maps and directories is available from leading book stores and stationers.

MARLBOROUGH SOUNDS MARITIME PARK: Based in one of New Zealand's most popular and beautiful holiday areas, this park at the northern tip of the South Island was established in 1953. Its region stretches from Cape Soucis in the west to Rarangi in the south-east and includes appropriate island reserves.

MORIORIS: The name given to some of the earlier Polynesian in-habitants of New Zealand. Although the term has been applied loosely in the past, it is now regarded as referring only to the in-habitants of the Chatham Islands. The Morioris were either killed or assimilated by later arrivals. In spite of hoary tales of supposed physical differences between Maori and Moriori, they are today regarded as related Polynesian peoples. Maori culture is considered to have developed continuously from the arrival of the first groups of people.

MOUNTAINS: New Zealand is a mountainous country. Less than one quarter of the land mass lies below the 200m contour. Although the South Island is more rugged than the North, the North Island's four highest peaks are volcanic cones, only one of which can be classed as dormant. They are Ruapehu (2797m), Egmont (2518), Ngauruhoe (2290), and Tongariro (1968). While Egmont is dormant, Ruapehu and Ngauruhoe still have periods of activity. Other vol-canic peaks are Tarawera (which erupted with disastrous conse-quences in the last century) and White Island. In the South Island, the massive chain of the Southern Alps includes many peaks higher than 3000m. The two highest bear the names of the first Euro-pean explorers to sight New Zealand. Mt Cook is 3766m high and

Mt Tasman some 3500m. Other major peaks are: Dampier 3440, Silberhorn 3279, Lendenfeld 3201, Hicks 3183, Malte Brun 3176, Torres 3163, Teichelmann 3160, Sefton 3157, Haast 3138, Elie de Beaumont 3109, Douglas Peak 3081, La Perouse 3079, Haidinger 3066, Minarets 3066, Aspiring 3036, Hamilton 3022, and Glacier Peak 3007.

NATIONAL PARKS: See parks

NEWSPAPERS: Each of the four main centres — Auckland, Wellington, Christchurch, and Dunedin — has a morning and evening newspaper which publishes daily except on Sunday. There are 27 daily newspapers in smaller centres. In addition there is a large number of newspapers publishing once or several times a week in smaller towns or city suburbs. In Auckland, the morning newspaper is the *New Zealand Herald* (the largest daily circulation in the country) and the evening paper is the *Auckland Star*. The Auckland-based tabloid, *Sunday News*, has the largest Sunday circulation in New Zealand. Wellington's morning newspaper is the *Dominion* and the afternoon paper, published by the same company, is the *Evening Post*. The *Sunday Times* is based here too. The Christchurch morning newspaper is *The Press* and the evening paper is the *Star* which has links with the Auckland evening paper. Dunedin has the *Otago Daily Times* each morning and the *Evening Star*.

PARKS: New Zealand has 10 national parks which make up about 13 per cent of the country's total land area. The status of a national park can be changed only by an Act of Parliament. In addition there are 981 scenic reserves, 80 historic reserves, 65 reserves for the preservation of fauna and flora, two maritime parks, many wildlife sanctuaries and refuges, and 866 public domains. The national park system began in 1877 when Te Heuheu Tukino and other Maori chiefs gifted to the Crown the summits of their sacred mountains, Ruapehu, Ngauruhoe, and Tongariro. These provided the nucleus of the Tongariro National Park which was established in 1894. The parks are listed below as described in the Government publication, the New Zealand Official Yearbook (Note: All but the first three parks named are in the South Island.):

Urewera National Park (199,994 hectares, established in 1954), surrounds the beautiful Lakes Waikaremoana and Waikareiti. As the traditional home of the Tuhoe, "the Children of the Mist", it is rich in Maori history. The park protects the largest remaining area of native forest in the North Island and provides a home for many species of native birds.

Tongariro National Park (70,087 hectares, established in 1894), includes the three active volcanic cones of Ruapehu, Ngauruhoe, and Tongariro. Ruapehu's snowfields are the winter playground of the North Island. Lake Rotopounamu, still free from exotic fish, and Mount Pihanga are two other focal points of the park.

Egmont National Park (33,527 hectares, established in 1900), contains one of the world's most symmetrical mountains, known to the Maoris as "Taranaki", and preserves magnificent scenery and vegetation within a 9 kilometre radius of the summit. Dominating Taranaki province in the west of the North Island, the near perfect cone varies from heavily-forested lower slopes to the bare scoria, rock, snow, and ice at the upper levels.

Abel Tasman National Park (20,085 hectares, established in 1942), with a broken coastline and rich in historical significance, has numerous tidal inlets and beaches of golden sand fronting Tasman Bay. Botanically, the park is unique as its bush-clad slopes show a blending of the natural cover of both the North and South Islands, a phenomenon of nature not found elsewhere in the country.

Nelson Lakes National Park (57,442 hectares, established in 1956), is named after the chief focal points for visitors, the beautiful lakes Rotoiti and Rotoroa. These nestle in rugged mountainous country with extensive beech-forest clad lower slopes. The Mount Robert area, with its magnificent views, provides visitors with winter recreational opportunities on its ski fields.

Arthur's Pass National Park (98,399 hectares, established in 1929), is a rugged and mountainous area straddling the main divide of the Southern Alps. It is an area of high peaks (at least 30 over 1800 metres), snowfields, deep-cut valleys, snow-grass clad ridges, forest-clad hillsides, high waterfalls, wide shingle riverbeds, and rushing torrents, all providing endless scope for physical endeavour or quiet appreciation.

Mount Cook National Park (69,958 hectares, established in 1953) and **Westland National Park** (88,608 hectares, established in 1960), share a common boundary along the main divide of the Southern Alps. Their magnificent alpine scenery containing almost all of the 27 peaks over 3,050 metres includes New Zealand's highest, the 3,764 metre Mount Cook, known to the Maoris as "Aorangi" — freely translated as "Cloud Piercer". Their attractions are as varied as their altitude, ranging from well known glaciers such as Tasman (at 29km long one of the longest outside polar regions), Franz Josef, and Fox, to hot springs, placid lakes, and the sub-tropical luxuriance of the rain forests.

Mount Aspiring National Park (287,206 hectares, established in 1964), is a complex of impressive glaciated mountain scenery which includes the headwaters of seven major rivers. The park's distinctive character is enhanced by bush-covered mountainside and pleasant river flats and valleys. It focal point, often referred to as the Matterhorn of New Zealand, is the 3,036 metre Mount Aspiring, a four ridged peak rising from the Bonar Therma-Volta ice shelf, and the country's highest peak outside Mount Cook National Park. **Fiordland National Park** (1,288,348 hectares, established in 1952), is one of the larger national parks in the world, and is re-nowned for the rugged grandeur of its scenery which includes fiords, mountains, forests, waterfalls, and lakes. The better known lakes are Manapouri, backed by snow-capped peaks, and Te Anau. The park is the only known habitat of two flightless birds, the takahe *(notornis)* and the kakapo.

PAUA: A large edible shellfish of the abalone family. The shells, when polished, display vivid marblings of colour and are much prized as jewellery and for souvenir items.

POLICE: New Zealand's police force has been modelled on the British system. Policemen do not carry guns, but there is a special armed offenders squad for dealing with emergencies in which firearms are involved. Traffic control is generally carried out by special traffic officers employed either by the larger local bodies or the Ministry of Transport.

POPULATION: By world standards, New Zealand's population is small — 3.1 million. Projections to the year 2000 show that the population is still likely to be less than 5 million. Of the present population, more than 70 per cent live in the North Island. Maoris make up about 8 per cent of the total population. Major settled areas are: Auckland, urban population 746,440, total for region 796,660; Hamilton, urban 96,690, total 152,740; Napier-Hastings, Napier urban 50,350, Hastings urban 51,180, total for region 109,360; Palmerston North, urban 62,870, total 87,000; Wellington, combined urban (includes Hutt Valley and Porirua) 333,710, total 354,660; Christchurch, urban 297,860, total 326,410; Dunedin, urban 114,410, total 120,890.

QUEENSTOWN: A major tourist centre on the shores of Lake Wakatipu in the South Island. Its population of 2,760 increases many times over during holiday seasons. The district offers boating, fishing, skiing, hiking, and visits to areas of historic or scenic interest.

RADIO: The Broadcasting Council of New Zealand, through Radio New Zealand, provides a network of 52 medium wave broadcasting stations and two short-wave transmitters. Twenty one stations maintain a daily 24-hour service. There are seven privately-owned commercial stations, the first of which, Radio Hauraki, began as a "pirate station" broadcasting from a ship off the coast of Auckland. The private stations are: Radio Hauraki (Auckland), Radio i (Auckland), Radio Waikato (Hamilton), Radio Whakatane, Radio Otago (Dunedin), Radio Avon (Christchurch), and Radio Windy (Wellington). The only private non-commercial station has been operated in Dunedin since 1922 by the Otago Radio Association Inc.

RAILWAYS: Both Islands are well-served by railway systems. Special services in the North Island are provided by the Silver Star overnight expresses between Auckland and Wellington, the Northerner express, and the Silver Fern diesel-electric rail car. In the South Island, the Southerner express operates between Christchurch and Invercargill. All except the Silver Fern have buffet or dining cars. The Silver Star expresses have air-conditioned sleeping cars.

RELIGION: The two main religious professions in New Zealand are Anglican (Church of England) and Presbyterian. Together they account for more than 50 per cent of the population. About 15 per cent of the population is Catholic. Other major religions are: Methodist, Baptist, Church of Jesus Christ of Latter Day Saints (Mormons), Ratana (a Maori church), Brethren, Salvation Army.

SKIING: The major developed ski-resorts in New Zealand are at Mt Ruapehu in the Tongariro National Park, Mt Egmont in the Taranaki province, Mt Cook National Park in the Southern Alps and Coronet Peak about 19km (12 miles) from Queenstown in the South Island's lake district. There are many smaller areas popular for skiing and vast areas which have been marked for future development.

SOUTHERN ALPS: The range of mountains extending roughly north-south for much of the length of the South Island. It includes most of New Zealand's highest peaks.

SPEED LIMITS: Cars in New Zealand are right-hand drive which means you will be driving on the left side of the road. While speed limits may vary according to circumstances, those applying over most of the country are: Open road, 80 kilometres an hour; urban areas, 50km/h. In limited speed zones, the maximum speed may be either 50km/h or 80km/h depending on the circumstances.

STAMPS: Postage stamps came into use in New Zealand in 1855 and proved an immediate success — both with the mail service and with stamp collectors. The New Zealand Royal Philatelic Society was formed in 1888 and today there are some 26 affiliated societies well served with catalogues and expertise. So busy were stamp sales that the first successful stamp vending machine was invented by the New Zealanders R.J. Dickie and J.H. Brown. After trials in 1905 the machines were installed in 1909 and world patents applied for. The four main centres have busy philatelic bureaus and there is a smaller one operating at Hamilton. Visitors can buy current New Zealand stamps and those of Western Samoa and the Tokelau Islands. The bureaus sell first day covers on the day of issue and for eight days afterwards. Visitors can fill out order forms for the first day covers if they wish and be put on the mailing list for advice on new stamps and services. The main bureau for overseas orders is at Wanganui and the address is Post Office Philatelic Bureau, Private Bag, Wanganui, New Zealand.

STEWART ISLAND: The third-largest island in the New Zealand group, with an area of 1,746 square kilometres. It is situated at the foot of the South Island and according to Maori legend was the anchor stone of the canoe (South Island) from which the hero, Maui, fished up the North Island.

TASMAN, Abel Janszoon (1606-59): Dutch explorer who was the first European to sight New Zealand. In 1642, the council of the East-India Company in Java sent Tasman with two small ships to explore southern waters. His main task was to see if a sea passage existed to South America. He sailed down the west coast of Australia (which was known to Dutch ships) and then followed the southern coast until discovering the island now known as Tasmania. On December 13, 1642, he sighted a "large and high land" — the west coast of the South Island. He followed the coast north and rounded the tip of the North Island without discovering the true nature of what he called Staten Landt. At Golden Bay he lost four men in a skirmish with Maoris, the first of many unfortunate experiences between Maori and Pakeha.

TELEVISION: New Zealand has two television channels broadcasting on the PAL 625-line colour system. Television One has its headquarters at Avalon Centre in Lower Hutt (near Wellington) and may be toured by the public (telephone first). Television Two, or South Pacific Television, is based in Auckland and as the newer service is still extending its operations. Both channels are required by the Broadcasting Council of New Zealand to have a local programme content of not less than 30 per cent.

THERMAL ACTIVITY: New Zealand's best-known area of thermal activity is at Rotorua in the North Island. There are many other hot pools, spas, and isolated pockets of activity in both islands. At Wairakei near Lake Taupo, geothermal steam has been harnessed to generate electricity.

WAITANGI: One of the most important areas of New Zealand historically. On February 6, 1840, the Treaty of Waitangi was signed between the British and paramount Maori Chiefs. Today the location at the Bay of Islands is preserved as a historical monument. Thousands of visitors inspect the Treaty House, the former Residency, each year. The building has been restored in as close to its original condition as possible and contains many relics dating back to 1832. Nearby is a whare runanga national Maori centennial memorial containing outstanding examples of decorative art. Visitors can also see a huge war canoe capable of carrying 80 warriors. Waitangi is a fully-developed tourist area and has some of New Zealand's most beautiful coastline scenery.

WAITOMO CAVES: The collective name given to a group of world famous glowworm caves in the North Island about 75 kilometres west of Hamilton and 155 miles south-west of Rotorua. Waitomo Cave is noted for its lofty chambers, deep shafts and fabulous glowworm grotto, regarded as one of the modern wonders of the world. Ruakuri Cave and the Aranui Caves, each with their own special attractions, complete the group.

WELLINGTON: The capital of New Zealand, and the centre of government and diplomatic activity. Wellington is a major port, the beautiful harbour being used by ships of all sizes, including inter-island vehicular and rail ferries connecting with Picton in the South Island. There is much to do and see in Wellington and many reminders of New Zealand's history. There is the Dominion Museum and the National Art Gallery in Buckle Street, a fine zoo, world-renowned botanical gardens, and appealing coastal drives and walks. Well worth a visit is the Alexander Turnbull Library, a national repository which grew from a private collection. A favourite outing for visitors is a ride by cable car from Lambton Quay to Kelburn, either to admire the fine views of the harbour or visit the botanical gardens. Wellington's many interesting buildings range from the old wooden Government building erected in 1876 and reputed to be one of the largest of its kind in the world, to the modern beehive-shaped replacement designed by the noted British architect, Sir Basil Spence. With its neighbouring cities of Upper Hutt, Lower Hutt and the Borough of Petone, Wellington is also a major industrial area. It was named after the "Iron Duke", the Duke of Wellington, who defeated Napoleon at the Battle of Waterloo, and who interested himself in the early settlement of New Zealand. At first Wellington was near Petone, but activites later shifted to Lambton Harbour around which the modern port area has developed. A great deal of land was reclaimed from the sea and visitors are often amused that major commercial streets, which are today some distance from the water, still retain their original names — Lambton Quay, Thorndon Quay, and Custom-house Quay.